The Innsmouth Tabernacle Choir Hymnal

by Brother Darrell Schweitzer

with an introduction
by the Rev. J. Apocalypse Gibber, Jr.
(Doctor of Inhumane Letters, Leng University)

Illustrated by Allen Koszowski

Zadok Allen: Publisher, 2004

The Innsmouth Tabernacle Choir Hymnal

by Brother Darrell Schweitzer

with an introduction
by the Rev. J. Apocalypse Gibber, Jr.
(Doctor of Inhumane Letters, Long University)

Illustrated by Allen Koszowski

WILDSIDE PRESS

Dedication:
For the Rev. Robert M. Price,
Hierophant of the Horde, and inspiration to us all.

CONTENTS

INTRODUCTION

Can you get down for Cthulhu, brothers and sisters? Can you *tremble* with the glory and power of the Old Ones? Do you want to give your self over, body and soul, to some ancient and tentacled entity conjured up out of the *Necronomicon* of Abdul Alhzared or even the New York phone directory?

Does the prospect of the hideous and agonizing doom of mankind, when the Earth shall be wiped clean and the Great Old Ones shall once again filter down from the stars, make you want to *get up and sing?*

If not, then on that day most likely you will be *lunch*, but otherwise, brothers and sisters, O Children of the Shadows, Hierophants of the Nameless, you are *one of us* and this book is for you. We of the Esoteric Order of Dagon (now Reformed since the Great Tribulation of 1927 which is described by H.P. Lovecraft in "The Shadow Over Innsmouth") hold to a very simple, straight-forward, and wholesome belief, which may be summed up in a few words: The Old Ones were, the Old Ones are, and the Old Ones shall be. Not in the spaces we know, but *between* them, they walk serene and primal, undimensioned and to us unseen.

But if that is the case, you may reasonably ask, what have the Old Ones got to do with me? How can *I* ever call upon them, when I have (quite sensibly) concluded that life is a hideous thing and maybe good old Planet Earth needs to be sterilized?

Well, you could always whistle, or better yet, attend eldritch and unspeakable Cthulhu Prayer Breakfasts such as the Reverend Robert M. Price used to conduct so brilliantly at the Necronomicon conventions in Providence, Rhode Island every summer, and join hundreds of believers like yourself chowing down on high-cholesterol foods (what or *who* is in the sausage?) and chanting the dark liturgies of Yeb and Nug.

You could also sing some of the songs in this book, most of which have been performed under such circumstances. But they're work anywhere, in the shower, or wherever they might reverberate through the mad abyss of the blind and meaningless cosmos.

Every little bit helps.

Brother Darrell has attended those Cthulhu Prayer Breakfasts. The spirit has moved him to witness Cthulhu before the assembled multitude. He once performed several of the hymns in this book in the company of Ms. Faye Wringel on the piano and the members of the Innsmouth Tabernacle Choir, each in their own, individual key. Brother Darrell has received these lyrics telepathically from out of the abyss. He has written them down. Now, with the help of one of Innsmouth's most venerable citizens, he has published them. Hallelujah! Iä! Shub-Niggurath! What more can anyone say? Brother Darrell is not nearly as inspiring in person as the Reverend Price, but still he is a faithful and diligent member of the Horde, a credit to the post-human race. He is actually one of our younger acolytes, being less than a full century in age. He has not yet begin the Change, but I can assure you, he already has the "look," and there is no question that he hears the music.

Dagon saves, brothers and sisters. He truly does. Everyone else shall be eaten. Won't you join us at the feast?

— Rev. J. Apocalypse Gibber, Jr.
Doctor of Inhumane Letters, Leng University

7

Cthulhu Loves His Loyal Minions

Cthulhu loves his loyal minions
gibb'ring out his eldritch praise!
We are gathered in his name
orgiastic without shame,
knowing R'lyeh will rise up one of these days.

Cthulhu's calling all his buddies,
summoned to Earth from outer spheres,
all the shoggoths and night-gaunts,
ghouls and leather-wingèd haunts,
that we recognize from dreams and primal fears.

Cthulhu devours all his minions!
Eternal death shall set us free!
As he stirs us in the broth
that is known as Azathoth,
Crawling Chaos will transfigure you and me!

Give Me That Old One Religion

chorus:
Give me that Old One Religion!
Give me that Old One Religion!
Give me that Old One Religion!
It's good enough for me!

It was good for Wizard Whateley,
though we haven't seen him lately;
much less fun for poor old Akeley
but it's good enough for me!

(chorus)

The Old Ones frightened Peaslee,
though I think he scared too eas'ly —
An old autograph, that's measly!
But it's good enough for me!

(chorus)

In a place far underground
Pickman's pals are gathered 'round,
making lunch of folks they've found.
That's good enough for me!

(chorus)

In Cthulhu we are trusting,
though his rites are quite disgusting;
from his crypt he'll soon be busting,
and that's good enough for me!

(and so on and so on until the stars are right.)

Eldritch Gifts

It's a gift to be squamous,
it's a gift to have fins,
it's a gift to have gills
when Cthulhu wins.
When all the stars are right,
on the world's last night,
we will swim in the glory of R'lyeh's light.

When our transformation's done,
we are the ones who will have all the fun.
When mankind's at an end,
as the Elder Ones descend,
we minions will rise to devour **and rend**.

It's a gift brought to us
from a weird, wild clime,
from a black-litten world at
the edge of space and time,
fulfilling all that's promised
in the *Necronomicon* —
These are the gifts of the Master's dawn.

*(Repeat in a slow and stately cadence, with slurping, flopping,
cries of "Iä!" and "Cthulhu fhtagn!" and cacodaemonic
cackling as appropriate.)*

What A Friend We Have in Dagon

What a friend we have in Dagon!
Let us swim to Devil Reef!
Shed our human forms forever,
for our stay on Earth is brief.

There we'll dwell in wondrous glory,
in many-columned Y'ha-nthlei,
reunited with our loved ones
who transformed in days gone by.

And when all the stars are right,
when sunken R'lyeh breaks the waves,
when Cthulhu gobbles mankind,
we shall know that Dagon saves!

An Eldritch Horror is Our God

An eldritch horror is our god,
who dwells beyond the curves of space.
Though some folks think this rather odd,
we gladly serve the Elder Race,

whose minions claimed the Earth
long years before our birth.
Again they shall return
and mankind's cities burn.

Let us praise then Azathoth,
and soon we'll see the world cleared off.
Lord of Chaos, primal broth,
devour all those who dare to scoff.

And then we faithful few
in death are born anew,
to gibber mindlessly
for all eternity.

Yes, They'll Take Our Brains to Yuggoth

Yes, they'll take our brains to Yuggoth,
to beautiful, methane-frozen Yuggoth.
Yes, they'll take our brains to Yuggoth,
to rest in the cold and the dark.

And when they've taken us to Yuggoth
and we whisper in the shadows and the quiet
with our bodies left so far behind us,
we'll forget that stupid Atkins diet.

Won't you come with us to Yuggoth?
A vacation unlike any other,
in canisters of shiny metal,
we will rest on a shelf in the dark.

Crawling Chaos Come for Me

Crawling Chaos, come for me!
Let my soul devoured be!
Let the mad auroras roll!
Let the doom of mankind toll,
while the seas with noxious birth,
unleash the powers 'neath the earth!

Let us praise Nyarlathotep!
Let's put some shamble in our step!
Like the beasts that lick his hands,
we shall grovel in the sands,
till crushing what he made in play
Chaos blows Earth's dust away!

Hymn to Yog-Sothoth

We sing of Yog-Sothoth
who dwells between the spaces!
Yog-Sothoth is the gate
for all the elder races,
which walk the Earth unseen
dread, primal, and serene,
and broke through once of old
just as Alhazred told.

Yog-Sothoth is the gate
the way between dimensions!
To call the Old Ones back,
we show our good intentions,
by bloody sacrifice,
nude orgies, very nice,
which maketh foulness sweet,
until the spheres shall meet.

I Have a Little Idol
(for children)

I have a little idol.
It's made of Innsmouth clay.
It looks like Lord Cthulhu.
Let's summon him today!

Iä! Lord Cthulhu!
He'll wipe the Earth quite clean.
Iä! Lord Cthulhu!
We think that's really keen.

My idol it is thirsty,
and when the stars are right,
we'll sacrifice a virgin,
and dance all through the night!

(repeat chorus)

ALLEN X. '86

Onward Dagon's Minions

Onward Dagon's minions
shambling as to war,
with the light of R'lyeh
shining as before!

Rise ye Dagon's minions
forth from Devil Reef
the reign on earth of mankind
shall thankfully be brief!

Humans ate my grandaddy,
they caught him in their nets,
sold him as fake crabmeat
or else as chow for pets.

Gather Dagon's minions
thousandfold and more!
It's time to eat the humans
and even up the score!

Notes

The newly-converted may need to be reminded of the blasphemous resemblances between some of our sacred hymns and certain effusions of the "normals." This is particularly true of the melodies, which were of course composed before the beginning of human history by the daemon-sultan Azathoth, but which are unfortunately better known in their corrupted forms. The relationships are as shown.

"Cthulhu Loves His Loyal Minions" = "Jesus Loves the Little Children."
"Give Me That Old One Religion" = "Give Me That Old-Time Religion."
"Eldritch Gifts" = "Simple Gifts."
"What A Friend We Have in Dagon" = "What A Friend We Have in Jesus."
"An Eldritch Horror Is Our God" = "A Mighty Fortress is Our God" (with no apologies whatsoever to Martin Luther).
"Yes, They'll Take Our Brains to Yuggoth" = "Yes, We'll Gather At the River."
"Crawling Chaos Come for Me" = "Rock of Ages."
"Hymn to Yog-Sothoth" = "Now Thank We All Our God."
"I Have a Little Idol" = "The Dreidel Song."
"Onward Dagon's Minions" = "Onward Christian Soldiers."

Pronunciation key: While many of the words in our liturgy are in the Elder Speech and therefore never intended for human speech organs, those faithful who have already made the Change should have no problem. But for novices, we recommend the following pronunciations to help control the level of gibbering cacophony — not that we have anything against gibbering cacophony, but there is a time, a place, and a decibel level for everything!

Cthulhu = "Cuth-ul-hoo" or "Kut-ul-hoo."
R'lyeh = "Rill-yeh!"
Y'ha-nthlei = "Yanith-Lye."

www.ingramcontent.com/pod-product-compliance
Lightning Source LLC
Chambersburg PA
CBHW021124020426
42331CB00004B/617